For Jay and Nigel

THE ELEM

1. FIRE

OBERT HINCHLIFFE

Printed in Great Britain
OXFORD UNIVERSITY PRESS, MUSIC DEPARTMENT, GREAT CLARENDON STREET, OXFORD OX2 6DP

15
mf
mp
18
21
f
24
dim.
dim.
p
p
28
p

32
p
37
p
42
p
47
mf
mf
52
mp
mp
mf
mf

57
sempre crescendo
mf
f
a tempo
61
ad lib.
lunga
lunga
8va ad lib.
ff
p
65
p
cresc. molto
69
martellato
72

76
79
82
mf
mf
86
mp
dim.
dim.
mp
90
senza rit.
8va
p
p
dim.
pp
pp

2. WATER

Tranquillo (♩ = 92)
Flute
Harpsichord or Piano
p cantabile
p
5
rit.
9
a tempo
pochiss. rit.
smorzando
mp
rubato
mp
cresc.
mf
dim.
14
a tempo
rit.
mp
mp
cresc.
dim.

a tempo
18
p
p
22
poco rit.
26
a tempo
molto rit.
a tempo
poco cresc.
dim.
30
poco stringendo
rall.
rit.
mp cresc.
mf
dim.
p
mp cresc.
mf
dim.
p
34
a empo
molto rit.
a tempo
p
poco cresc.
dim.

poco stringendo
rall.
molto rit.
38
ten.
mp cresc.
mf dim.
ten.
ten.
ten.
42
a tempo
pochiss. rit.
mp
mp cresc.
mf dim.
46
a tempo
rit.
mp
mp
cresc.
mf
50
a tempo
p
p
54
calando

Robert Hinchliffe

The Elements

Flute

Oxford University Press

For Jay and Nigel

THE ELEMENTS

FLUTE

1. FIRE

ROBERT HINCHLIFFE

Printed in Great Britain
OXFORD UNIVERSITY PRESS, MUSIC DEPARTMENT, GREAT CLARENDON STREET, OXFORD OX2 6DP

40
45
mf
50
mp
55
mf
sempre crescendo
59
f
ad lib.
ff
lunga
lunga
a tempo
8va ad lib.
p
64
2
1
1
5
75
f
79
82
mf
3
89
mp
dim.
senza rit.
p
1
8va
pp

2. WATER

Tranquillo (♩ = 92)
p cantabile
rit.
smorzando
a tempo
mp
pochiss. rit.
a tempo
mp
rit.
a tempo
p
poco rit.
a tempo
molto rit.
a tempo
poco stringendo
mp cresc.
mf dim.
rall.
rit.
p
a tempo
molto rit.
a tempo
poco stringendo
mp cresc.
rall.
mf dim.
molto rit.
ten.
a tempo
mp
pochiss. rit.
a tempo
mp
rit.
a tempo
p
calando

3. EARTH

Tempo giusto (♪ = 108)
f
ff
Andante (♪ = 88)
rall.
mf
mp
poco cresc.
poco stringendo . . . . Tempo I
pp
p
rall.
attacca

4. AIR

Prestissimo, scherzando e giocoso (♩. = 152)
f sempre leggiero
6
11
1
p
16
1
p
f
21
26
8va
3
p
33
3
f
sub. p
40
f
sub. p
1
45
mp
1
mp
p

Printed by Caligraving Limited Thetford Norfolk England

3. EARTH

Tempo giusto (♪ = 108)
Flute
Harpsichord
or Piano
f
f
10
16
22
dim.
ff

28
33
ff
5
38
rall.
mf
mf
dim.
Andante (♪ = 88)
43
mp
mp
poco cresc.
48

poco stringendo . . . . Tempo I
pp
p
p
rall.
attacca

4. AIR

Prestissimo, scherzando e giocoso (♩. = 152)
Flute
Harpsichord or Piano
f sempre leggiero
f
p
p
p
cresc.

18
f
f
23
27
8va
ff
sub.p
p
32
ff
sub.p
cresc.
36
f
sub.p
p
f
f

41
sub. p
mp
p
mp
46
mp
p
p
mp
50
p
p
f
55
mf
f
dim.
60
mp
mp

64
mf
cresc.
69
dim.
mf
mf
mp
74
mp
p
p
78
pp
pp
82
pp

Printed by Caligraving Limited Thetford Norfolk England